Purbeck

by Robert Westwood

Second edition

ISBN 978-0-9564104-7-4

Contains Ordnance Survey data © Crown copyright and database right (2011)

Reprinted 2019 and 2023

Inspiring Places Publishing

2 Down Lodge Close

Alderholt

Fordingbridge

Hampshire

SP6 3JA

www.inspiringplaces.co.uk

Contents

Below are listed the pages with walks that satisfy one or more of the following criteria.

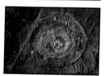
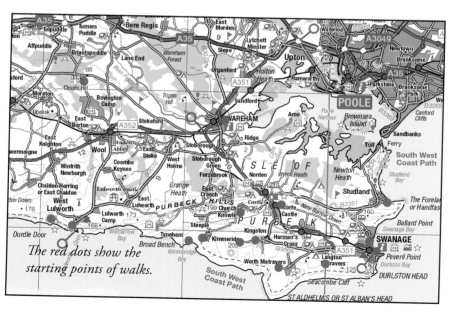

The red dots show the starting points of walks.

Introduction

For the walker, Purbeck has it all - stunning coastline, picturesque villages, rolling countryside and more than its fair share of history. Combine this with a wonderful variety of places to stay; from luxury hotels to bed and breakfast accommodation with real character; high quality self-catering and beautiful camp sites; and you have the perfect location for a walking holiday.

This guide details twenty walks that show off this tremendous variety. As well as giving clear descriptions of the walks it also presents information about the different localities - including history and the amazing geological story of the world-famous Jurassic Coast.

All the walks can be found on the Ordnance Survey Outdoor Leisure map OL15. You are strongly recommended to use this - the maps in the book are intended only as rough guides.

All the walks are suitable for dogs, but please be careful near cliffs, especially on the walks on pages 4, 10, 14, 22, 24, 27, 30, 31and 32. Remember to take plenty of water, for yourselves and the dog(s) and please keep dogs under close control near farm animals.

For pushchairs and wheelchair users I would suggest making use of the paths at Durlston Head, the seafront at Swanage and a visit to Tyneham where it is also possible to go down to Worbarrow Bay.

Every effort has been made to ensure the information in this book is correct at the time of going to press, but changes beyond our control may occur subsequently. If you have any observations to make or encounter any problems in the course of any of the walks please let us know through the website. (www.inspiringplaces.co.uk)

Although no specific walk has been detailed there, the Arne peninsula east of Wareham has a number of trails across the heathland and is an RSPB Nature Reserve. There is an information centre at the car park - (SY 971876, BH20 5BJ).

* The grid reference and nearest post code is given for each starting point.

Studland, Handfast Point and Ballard Down (SZ 038826, BH19 3AU)

Stunning cliffs, an intriguing churchyard and a quaint pub by the sea.

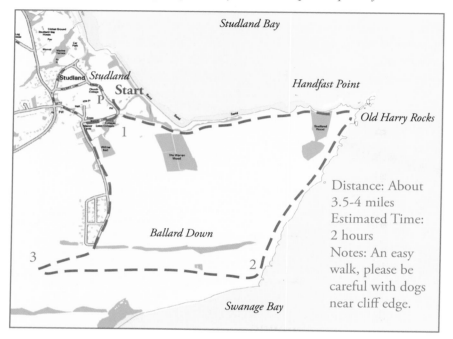

Distance: About 3.5-4 miles
Estimated Time: 2 hours
Notes: An easy walk, please be careful with dogs near cliff edge.

The walk starts at the National Trust car park alongside the Bankes' Arms. Walk past the pub, down the hill and turn left by the public conveniences at the bottom (1). Now follow the path all the way to Handfast Point and enjoy the magnificent views over Studland Bay to Poole and Bournemouth. The Chalk here represents the end of the Jurassic Coast; it also marks the end of the Cretaceous Period, and a turning point in the evolution of life when many species, including the dinosaurs, perished in the Great Extinction.

Follow the coast path south along the edge of the cliffs. You need to turn right along the Purbeck Way across Ballard Down, but if you ignore the first turning you can enjoy spectacular views over Swanage Bay before forking right to join the Purbeck Way (2). Carry on across the down, past a stone seat and then turn right at a signpost (3), following the path down to Studland. As it joins a road, turn right and follow it back to the car park.

Before you leave be sure to pay a visit to Studland Church. This lovely old building still has Saxon parts and near the front porch is the grave of Serjeant William Lawrence, a veteran of the Napoleonic Wars who became the landlord of the local inn after retiring. The grave details an extraordinary career; he fought in all the major battles of the Peninsular campaign before participating in the Battle of Waterloo.

Studland is a beautiful, secluded, tranquil spot and the Bankes' Arms is as good a place as any to seek refreshment after a walk. Alternatively try the National Trust café on the beach at Knoll Beach.

Above: The sea stacks of Old Harry and his family off Handfast Point. In the distance can be seen the coastline of Bournemouth and Christchurch. The Chalk was formed in shallow, tropical seas over 60 million years ago and consists almost entirely of microscopic shells formed by tiny algae.

Right: The gravestone of Sgt. Lawrence, telling his remarkable story.

Swanage to Corfe Castle (SZ 031796, BH19 1NY)
A quaint village, a fairy tale castle and a steam train.

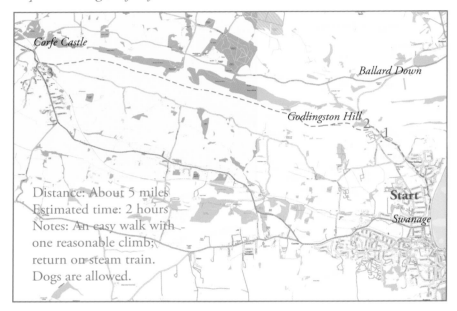

Corfe Castle

Ballard Down

Godlingston Hill

Start

Swanage

Distance: About 5 miles
Estimated time: 2 hours
Notes: An easy walk with
one reasonable climb;
return on steam train.
Dogs are allowed.

This is a one way walk along the Chalk ridge from Swanage to Corfe Castle. Enjoy some refreshment in one of the village's pubs or cafés before heading back on the famous steam railway. If you are a steam enthusiast check the timetable carefully; diesel trains are also used.

Walk north along the seafront at Swanage and continue along Ulwell Road. Follow this out of the town towards Studland. Continue past Ulwell Holiday Park (1) and just past a layby on the right hand side of the road. If you wish it is possible to park and start the walk here. Just past the layby on the other side of the road is a footpath (2). Go throught the gate, turn left and follow the path by the holiday park and up on to the Chalk ridge. This joins up with the Purbeck Way across Nine Barrow Down. Once on Nine Barrow Down follow the path along the top of the ridge all the way to Corfe Castle. Just before the village the path descends to a road (3). Follow this into the village.

The entrance to the station is down a small road almost opposite the square and the church. Trains back to Swanage are relatively frequent; check out the timetable at www.swanagerailway.co.uk or call 01929 425800.

Above: Corfe Castle viewed from the ridge.

The Saxons built a stronghold here, but it was probably of wooden construction. Viking raids were common and this natural isolated hill in the Chalk ridge made a perfect defensive position. It was here in AD 978 that the young King Edward was infamously murdered on the orders of his stepmother so that her son Ethelred (the Unready) could become king. After the Conquest the Normans began strengthening the castle and it grew in importance in the reign of King John, for whom it was a favourite hunting residence. It was besieged by King Stephen in the civil war with the Empress Matilda and later in the Civil War of the seventeenth century when it was gallantly held for the Royalists by Lady Bankes, whose husband Sir John Bankes was Attorney General but died suddenly in 1644. Lady Bankes led the defence of the castle for weeks until February 1646 when an act of betrayal let Parliamentarians into the stronghold. After the siege the castle was 'slighted', blown up with gunpowder, so that it could never be used as a stronghold again. Bear this in mind when looking at it – it is not the ravages of time that have done the damage!

Swanage and Durlston Country Park (SZ 033787, BH19 2LN)

Dramatic limestone coast and the legacy of a Victorian philanthropist.

Distance: About 3 miles
Estimated time: 1.5-2 hours
Notes: Allow time to explore Durlston Country Park, particularly the visitor centre.

Durlston Country Park was the creation of Victorian entrepreneur George Burt. He built the "castle" in 1887. It was never used as a home, but as a restaurant.

Walk south along the promenade, past the pier and continue along to Peveril Point (1). Follow the path up alongside the cliff edge of Durlston Bay to the top of the large grassy park. There is a convenient seat here from which to admire the view over Swanage Bay. The cliffs of Durlston Bay to your right (east) are of rocks from the Purbeck series and have yielded many fossils, including, in recent years, an ancient crocodile, a model of which is on display in the Durlston Visitor Centre. From here follow the path out on to the road (2) and walk alongside it south towards Durlston Head. You can turn off left into the woods and follow the path up to the headland. There are a number of paths to choose from but if you keep heading upwards you will not go wrong.

When you reach Durlston Head Country Park, stop to have a look around the visitor centre with its exhibitions on the Jurassic Coast and of local art. You might want to have a drink and a meal at the excellent café with stunning views over the sea (or save it for the way back). Continue along the coast path that hugs the top of the cliffs. You will come to the Tilly Whim caves, cut into the Portland Stone by quarrymen, and the Anvil Point lighthouse. Turn right by the lighthouse, across the small bridge (3) and follow the road back to the car park at Durlston Head. Follow the road out of the Country Park (please note there is a footpath to the right of the road) and turn right at Belle Vue Road (2). At the end follow the path down to Peveril Point and the starting point.

Above: The remains of the old Swanage pier, built to facilitate the export of stone.

Left: The Great Globe at Durlston Country Park. It was constructed in Greenwich in 1887 from Portland Stone and shipped to Swanage in 15 pieces.

Below: Tilly Whim caves on the south coast of Purbeck within Durlston Country Park.

Dancing Ledge and Seacombe (SY 997784, BH19 3HG)

Purbeck's stunning limestone coastline.

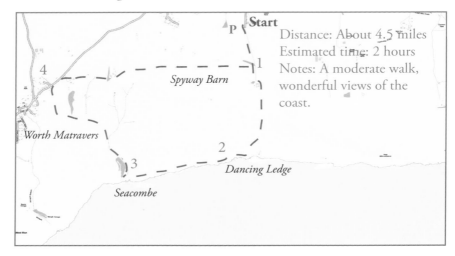

Start

Distance: About 4.5 miles
Estimated time: 2 hours
Notes: A moderate walk, wonderful views of the coast.

Spyway Barn

4

Worth Matravers

2

3

Dancing Ledge

Seacombe

This walk begins at a small National Trust car park at the end of Durnford Drove in Langton Matravers. From here follow the footpath south across the fields, past Spyway Barn (1) until you arrive at the top of a steep slope that leads down to the coast. You might want to stop and admire the view from here before heading down the path that takes you to Dancing Ledge below (2). It is well worth while going over the stile and down the steps to explore Dancing Ledge. This is another old quarrying site and its name derives from the action of waves over the flat rock surfaces.

The Purbeck coast.

Above: The Portland limestone was quarried here at Seacombe up until the Second World War. It was mainly extracted by tunneling into the cliffs.

Next retrace your steps to the coast path and follow it westwards as it clings to the top of the dramatic cliffs. At Seacombe (3) the path descends and turns inland to follow a valley northwards for a short while. Just after the bottom of the descent you will see a stile and a path that leads down to the old quarries at Seacombe. Again, this is worth exploring and is a great place to sit and watch the sea for a while and eat a picnic if you have one. Then rejoin the path heading up the valley. After a short while the path branches into two. Take the left fork over a small bridge across the stream. You will come to a fairly steep, but short, climb up the side of the valley. Take this, carry on across the field and over the stile at the end. Worth Matravers is across the valley in front of you – turn right and follow the side of the valley to the road. Turn right along the road and just after the end of the village take a footpath on the right leading across a field (4). At the other side of the field this joins the Priest's Way, a wide track that leads to Swanage. Look out for a sign on your left to Keates Quarry where you can view dinosaur footprints left in an ancient Jurassic lagoon (right). Then continue on the path which will take you just north of Spyway Barn where you should turn left back to the starting point.

Worth Matravers, Winspit and Seacombe (SY 974777, BH19 3LF)

Rugged cliffs and great views of the Purbeck coast.

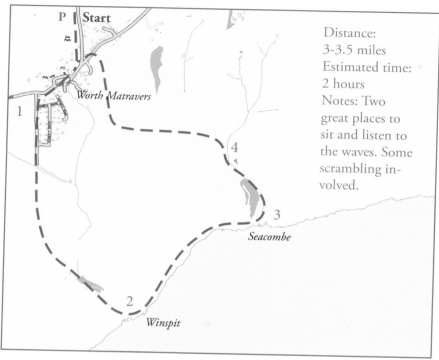

Distance:
3-3.5 miles
Estimated time:
2 hours
Notes: Two
great places to
sit and listen to
the waves. Some
scrambling in-
volved.

This lovely village is the perfect base for a number of walks. It is easy to get to by car or bus and has a great pub. Just below the duck pond is a small path leading past a row of cottages (1). Follow this and it will lead you to the sea at Winspit (2). This is a small cove that was once an important quarry in the Portland Stone. Huge caverns in the cliffs are a reminder of the difficult and dangerous work that once went on here. It is worth spending a little time exploring before continuing. A scramble down to the rocky shore will be enjoyed by youngsters – look out for the giant ammonite in the rocks. This is a species known as titanites, and is a 'zone fossil' for the Portland Stone. Also clearly visible are the remains of fossilised worm burrows and mollusc shells.

When you are ready follow the coast path to the east (left) of the cove which will take you to Seacombe (3). This was another quarry and you will need to go over a stile to the path leading down to the sea. This is a lovely, secluded place to sit and watch the sea – you may well have it all to yourself.

Take the path leading inland (north) back towards Worth Matravers. Fork left over a small bridge over the stream (4) and climb up the hill. When

you reach the top climb over the stile in the wall and turn right to follow the edge of the field. You will come to a gate by the road. Turn left and follow the road back to the car park or the Square and Compass.

Above: Waves batter the quarried shore at Winspit.

Middle: Note the large ammonite.

Right: The quarries at Winspit seen approaching from Seacombe. Portland Stone was quarried at Winspit until about 1940. In more recent times it has been used as a location for episodes of Doctor Who and for the Star Wars series Andor.

Worth Matravers, Winspit and around St. Aldhelm's Head

A dramatic headland of Portland Stone. (SY 974777, BH19 3LF)

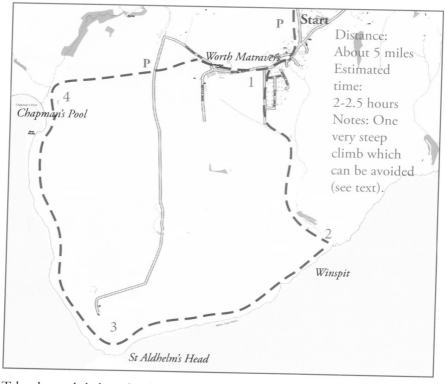

Distance: About 5 miles
Estimated time: 2-2.5 hours
Notes: One very steep climb which can be avoided (see text).

Worth Matravers

Chapman's Pool

Winspit

St Aldhelm's Head

Take the path below the duck pond in the centre of the village (1). It leads south by the side of a row of cottages to the sea at Winspit (2). Follow it all the way down and spend some time looking around this little cove that has been extensively quarried for Portland Stone. The path down to the water is a bit of a scramble, so be careful. Look out for the giant ammonite in the rocks near the water's edge (see previous walk). To the west of the cove are huge quarries blasted out of the cliffs. They can be explored at your own risk. When you have finished looking around here go back along the path a short way then take the coast path on the left that leads up to the top of the cliffs and follow this all the way round to St. Aldhelm's Head (3). Here you will find a memorial to the development of radar during the war; some key installations were on these cliffs. Take some time to look inside St. Aldhelm's Chapel, a tiny, but beautiful Norman church, probably built on the site of a much older place of worship. St. Aldhelm was the first Bishop of Sherborne in the eighth century and founded a number of churches around Dorset.

Above: The view westwards from St. Aldhelm's Head.

    Continue on the coast path around the headland – you will soon be rewarded with spectacular views along the Jurassic Coast to Kimmeridge and beyond. Rather annoyingly, the path descends into a steep valley and back up again; if you don't want to do this you can take the unmade road back to Worth Matravers beside the coastguard cottages, but you will miss out on the views!

    The coast path will take you by the side of Chapman's Pool; just past the cove take a footpath on the right (4) over the fields to a small car park. This is where the road past the coastguard cottages leads. Now follow the track, which soon turns into a metalled road, back to Worth Matravers. If you wish there is a path across a field through a farm which cuts a corner of the road off.

Right: Inside St. Aldhelm's Chapel.

Above: Looking across Chapman's Pool from the coast path with the Jurassic Coast stretching away westwards. On the far side of the bay Houns-tout is capped by Portland Stone.
Right: The village green and pond at Worth Matravers, a lovely village built from Purbeck Stone.

Left: A wall outside the famous 'Square and Compass'. This quaint old pub is very popular with walkers and is very atmospheric, both inside and out. It has its own, quite extensive, fossil collection, housed in a little museum on the side. Entrance is free.

Kimmeridge Bay (SY 918800, BH20 5NZ)

Great views from the ridge above Kimmeridge.

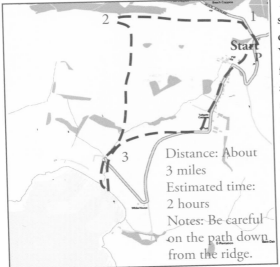

Distance: About 3 miles
Estimated time: 2 hours
Notes: Be careful on the path down from the ridge.

There is an old quarry by the side of the road on the ridge overlooking Kimmeridge. You can park here for free. Go back up the road away from Kimmeridge a short distance and take the second footpath sign on the left (1). Follow this path along the ridge from where there are lovely views over the bay. Just before a stile take the footpath on the left which leads down the side of the hill (2). Be careful down here, it can be a bit overgrown. After a short while take the path on the right signed Kimmeridge which will take you down across the fields to the sea. To return re-trace your steps but take the path on the right signed "Village and Etches Museum"(3). Follow this across along the side of the field. When you come to two footbridges take the right hand one, go through the gate and across the field to the road. Walk up the road to the church, go through the gate by the church and follow the path to Top Quarry and the car park. You might want to stop at Clavell's Café and visit the fossil museum (see page 25).

Going down to Kimmeridge from the limestone ridge.

Corfe Castle and Kingston (SY 958814, BH20 5HA)

Great views of the castle, a quaint village and a great pub garden.

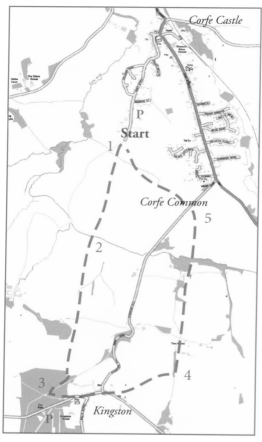

This walk starts at the southern end of West Street in Corfe Castle (1). (There is a car park along this street.) From here go south across Corfe Common (the 'Hardy Way'). Where the path forks keep right and follow it to the end of the common (follow signs for Kingston) (2). From here just keep following the path straight up the hill towards Kingston. (The church acts as a good marker.) When you reach a wooded path turn right and then immediately left (3). You will emerge by the Scott Arms, where you might want to relax in the lovely garden with tremendous views over Corfe Castle. Turn left as you leave the Scott Arms and right at the junction up the hill. Shortly after the old church take a path to the left across

Distance: About 3.5-4 miles

Estimated time: 2 hours

Notes: An easy walk but a moderate climb up the ridge to Kingston.

Right: The garden of the Scott Arms at Kingston.

Above: Corfe Castle from Corfe Common. Below: Kingston Church.

a field. Follow this path across three fields, keeping the fence on your left, until you reach a larger path (4). This is the Purbeck Way; turn left and follow the path alongside a small stream. Continue across Corfe Common, keeping left and you will reach a small road, the B3069 (5). Go across the road and through a gate onto the common again. Go across the common to the starting point (you will be able to see it).

Be sure to have a look at the church (right) before you leave Kingston. It was begun in 1874 by the 3rd Earl Eldon and completed in 1880. For many years it served as the private chapel for the Eldon family (see next walk) and was only consecrated as the parish church in 1921. It was designed by the famous architect George Street. The stone and marble for its construction was all quarried from the Eldon estate and it was built largely by local workers and craftsmen.

Kingston and Swyre Head   (SY 943793, BH20 5LP)

A gentle walk to a spectacular viewpoint.

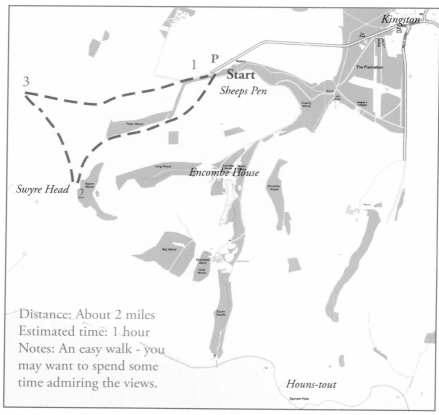

Distance: About 2 miles
Estimated time: 1 hour
Notes: An easy walk - you
may want to spend some
time admiring the views.

Follow the small road through the village of Kingston, past the Scott Arms and the 'new' church, and you will come to Sheeps Pen car park on the left of the road (1). Go through the gate at the back of the car park and follow the path up the hill. At the top of the hill the path passes by the side of a wood and leads to Swyre Head (2) from where there are wonderful views along the Jurassic Coast; to Kimmeridge and Lulworth to the west, and across to St. Aldhelm's Head to the east.

On the way up you will have good views over the "Golden Bowl" and the Encombe Estate. This ancient estate was bought by the Pitt family in 1734 and the fine house was built by John Pitt, a distant relative of the famous William Pitt(s). It was later bought by John Scott who, as Lord Eldon, greatly improved and extended the house. In 2009 an airline tycoon purchased the estate for around £20 million.

Above: The view west from Swyre Head.

On the other (west) side of Swyre Head is another fertile valley with a manor. This is Smedmore House and was built in the early seventeenth century by Sir William Clavell who was trying to develop a glassworks and other industries at Kimmeridge. The famous folly, Clavell Tower, was built about 1830 by Reverend John Richards who had changed his name to Clavell after inheriting the estate.

When you have had enough of the magnificent views walk inland alongside the wall to the west of Swyre Head; go through the next field and then at Heaven's Gate take a footpath on the right signed Kingston (3). This will lead back to the car park and to Kingston.

This lovely village is built almost entirely of Purbeck Stone, with most of the cottages dating from the nineteenth century. Be sure to have a look at the grand church (see previous walk).

Right: The Scott Arms.

Kingston, Rope Lake Head and Houns-tout (SY 954795, BH20 5LL)

Great views along the Jurassic Coast.

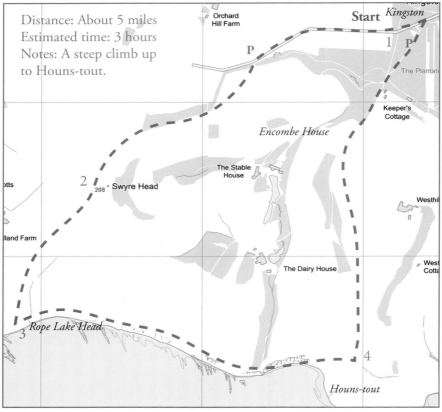

Distance: About 5 miles
Estimated time: 3 hours
Notes: A steep climb up
to Houns-tout.

There is a small car park in the woods on the road past the church (1). From here walk down the road to where the tarmac ends; go through the gate on the left and follow the path up to Swyre Head (2) (as previous walk). On the west side of the headland there is a stile; go over this and take a permissive path down to the sea at Rope Lake Head (3). Turn left at the coast and follow the coast path all the way up to Houns-tout (4). The last part of this is quite steep, but once here there are great views west towards Kimmeridge and east across to St. Aldhelm's Head.

From Houns-tout there is a path almost due north along the ridge. Take this and follow it back to the woods and the car park. On your left you will see the "Golden Bowl" and Encombe House (see previous walk).

Right: The view westwards from the top of Houns-tout.

Kingston, Rope Lake Head and Kimmeridge

Great views from the coast and the ridge. (SY 943793, BH20 5LP)

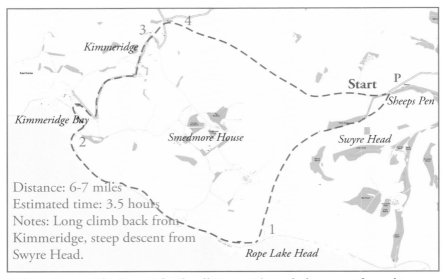

Distance: 6-7 miles
Estimated time: 3.5 hours
Notes: Long climb back from Kimmeridge, steep descent from Swyre Head.

Below: Kimmeridge Bay with Clavell Tower. The rocks here were formed in a Jurassic sea teeming with life. Look out for fossils in rocks on the beach.

We begin at the same parking place as on page 20 (Sheeps Pen). Follow the directions to Rope Lake Head (1) as on page 22. This time turn right along the coast path and head westwards towards Kimmeridge. The coast path hugs the top of the cliffs and affords some splendid views along the Jurassic Coast to Kimmeridge, Gad Cliff and beyond. Just before you reach Kimmeridge you will pass Clavell Tower (2), originally a folly built by Reverend John Richards in about 1830. Richards, who changed his name to Clavell after inheriting the Smedmore Estate, built the tower as a lookout and observatory. In recent years it has been moved brick by brick a little further inland because of cliff erosion and is currently a holiday home run by the Landmark Trust.

Carry on down the coast path to Kimmeridge Bay where you might want to stop a while and explore the beach. When you are ready follow the road out away from the beach and through the village. You will find refreshments at Clavell's Farm Shop and Café just before the church, and you can visit The Etches Collection opposite, a wonderful museum of Jurassic marine life. To save walking all the way up the road, take the small path past the churchyard (3) and follow it up the hill to where it joins the road once more. At the top of the hill turn right then immediately left up another small road (to Bradle) (4) and very shortly take the path on the right leading uphill. This follows the limestone ridge back towards Swyre Head. Before you reach there you will come to a gate named "Heaven's Gate"; turn left here following a path signed Kingston. This will lead back to the starting point.

Below: The coast path towards Kimmeridge from Rope Lake Head.

Kingston, Houns-tout and Hill Bottom (SY 954795, BH20 5LL)
The "Golden Bowl" and a delightful wooded valley.

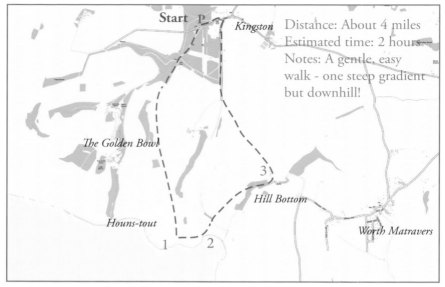

Start P — Kingston

Distance: About 4 miles
Estimated time: 2 hours
Notes: A gentle, easy
walk - one steep gradient
but downhill!

The Golden Bowl

3

Hill Bottom

Houns-tout

Worth Matravers

1   2

Follow the road in Kingston past the Scott Arms and the large church on the left. As the road enters a wood there is a (free) car park on the left. This is the start point for this walk. Take the footpath alongside the car park through the woods and follow it onto the grassy ridge on the east of the Encombe Valley, also known as the "Golden Bowl". Walk southwards along the ridge until you come to the coast at Houns-tout (1). From the ridge you will have good views of Encombe House (see page 20). Houns-tout cliff is capped by Portland and Purbeck limestone which accounts for its height; there are spectacular views west along the Jurassic Coast towards Kimmeridge (see page 23).

Now follow coast path to the left (east) and go down the steep path with steps towards Chapman's Pool. At the bottom turn left across a small stream (2) and walk towards the end of a tarmac lane that leads from Kingston. Turn right and follow the track around the side of the hill and up a small wooded valley. This leads to Hill Bottom and a collection of pretty cottages. When you reach the cottages turn left up the path (3) and follow it as it climbs gently up a narrow gully, which may be a bit overgrown depending on the time of year. The path soon opens out into fields; keep the dry stone wall on your right and you will reach a gate with a "permissive path" sign on the right. Take this path across the field and join the small tarmac road, turning right back towards Kingston and the starting point.

Kimmeridge, Worbarrow and Tyneham (SY 908791, BH20 5PE)

World famous geology and a deserted village.

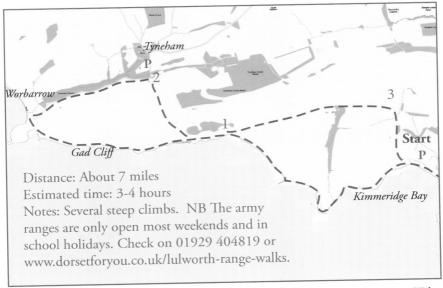

Distance: About 7 miles

Estimated time: 3-4 hours

Notes: Several steep climbs. NB The army ranges are only open most weekends and in school holidays. Check on 01929 404819 or www.dorsetforyou.co.uk/lulworth-range-walks.

The walk begins at the car park above the beach at Kimmeridge Bay. Take the steps down to the beach at the western end of the car park but instead of going down onto the beach take the path to the right that goes beside some cottages. The path goes past the 'nodding donkey' of the Kimmeridge oil well and through a gate that leads on to the army ranges. Now follow the path by the edge of the cliff all the way up to Tyneham Cap (1). On the way you will have wonderful views across Brandy Bay to Gad Cliff. As the name suggests, this was once a favourite spot for smugglers, whose accomplices hauled kegs of brandy up the cliffs after they had been landed on the narrow beach.

Keep close to the cliff edge and follow the path along to Worbarrow Bay. Be careful with dogs and children, the edge of the cliff is hidden and there is a long, sheer drop. Worbarrow Bay makes an ideal place to stop for a

Above: Post Office Row was the heart of Tyneham village. The refurbished telephone box stands outside the cottage that served as the Post Office. The cottages have now been made safe and all feature displays telling the story of those who lived in them. At the far end of the row is the church.

picnic. The steeply dipping layers of Purbeck limestone that form Worbarrow Tout at the southern end of the bay were formed in a shallow, coastal lagoon at the end of the Jurassic Period. When you are ready to leave Worbarrow, follow the path inland along the valley to the deserted village of Tyneham (above and next page). After exploring this lovely spot take the path up the hill where you entered the village (near Tyneham Farm) (2). Continue up to the top of Gad Cliff and instead of going back down the path you took earlier from Kimmeridge, follow the path up along the ridge. From this there are wonderful views over the bay and the Purbeck countryside to the north. Just before a gate at the end of the army ranges turn right (3) and follow the track down the fields back towards Kimmeridge. You will rejoin the original path just after the gate where you entered the ranges. Retrace your steps to the car park.

Be sure to go down to the beach this time and look for the many ammonites lying in the hard, flat limestone strata (see page 27). Why not "collect" some with your camera?

Worbarrow Bay (right) is carved out of soft Cretaceous sediments sandwiched between the harder ridges formed from the Portland and Purbeck limestones to the south and the Chalk to the north. These softer sediments were formed in a huge river delta at a time when  some of the largest dinosaurs roamed the Earth. Dinosaur footprints have been found in the Purbeck limestones of Worbarrow Tout at the southern end of the bay. As mentioned above, these limestones were deposited in shallow, coastal lagoons covered with dense vegetation and must have provided an ideal environment for some of the giant reptiles.

Tyneham was requisitioned by the army in December 1943 to prepare for the Normandy landings. The villagers were promised they could return after the war, but continuing military tension during the Cold War that followed meant this never happened. The ruined cottages, the still intact church and schoolhouse (with its charming museum) are a poignant memorial to a lost, rural way of life.

Above and right: The church and one of its stained glass windows.

Lulworth and Durdle Door (SY 822801, BH20 5RJ)

World famous geology.

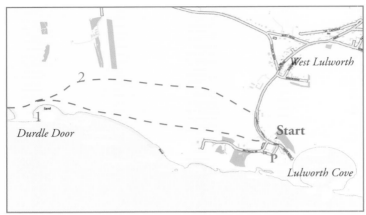

Distance: About 2 miles
Estimated time: 1-2 hours
Notes: A steep climb from Lulworth.

From the car park at Lulworth Cove take the coast path leading westwards up the hill. Folllow this all the way to Durdle Door (1) where you can descend some steps to the beach. On the way back keep to the left hand path towards the holiday park and at the grassy car park turn right over a stile (2) and follow the path back towards the cove across the top of the hill. You will emerge on the road that leads down to the cove. Cross the road to the footpath, turn right and follow the road back to the cove.

Durdle Door at dusk.

Durdle Door, Bat's Head and White Nothe (SY 809805, BH20 5RS)

A rollercoaster ride along the Chalk cliffs.

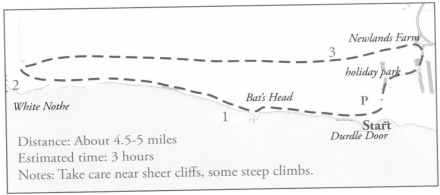

Distance: About 4.5-5 miles
Estimated time: 3 hours
Notes: Take care near sheer cliffs, some steep climbs.

From the car park just above Durdle Door follow the coast path westwards along the Chalk cliffs. The path includes some steep ascents and descents, passing first Swyre Head and then Bat's Head (1), the far headland in the photograph below. At West Bottom the path goes a little away from the cliff edge, past a Beacon (a tall stone pyramid). Just past here turn right inland on a path signed Dagger's Gate (2). Follow the path back along the ridge, keeping the fence to your left. Near the end take the path to Newland's Farm (3), keeping to the left of the dry valley of Scratchy Bottom. You will emerge on the road by the entrance to the Durdle Door Holiday Park. Follow the road through the park back to the car park.

Below: The view west from Bat's Head.

Lulworth, Mupe Bay and Bindon Hill (SY 822800, BH20 5RH)
A Jurassic forest where dinosaurs roamed.

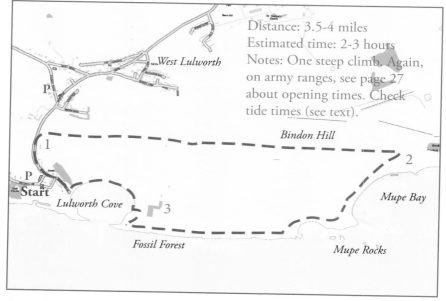

Distance: 3.5-4 miles
Estimated time: 2-3 hours
Notes: One steep climb. Again, on army ranges, see page 27 about opening times. Check tide times (see text).

From the Heritage Centre walk up the road away from the Cove. After the last cottage on your right (1) you will see a path leading up Bindon Hill. Take this, enter the army ranges, and at the top follow the path eastwards along the Chalk ridge. As you near the Chalk cliffs of Mupe Bay (2) you will see a path descending on your right. Follow this down to the bottom and if you wish go down the narrow path to the beach at Mupe Bay. This is a lovely quiet spot that you may have all to yourself. When you are ready continue along the coast path past Mupe Rocks and then westwards along the top of the limestone cliffs towards Lulworth Cove.

On your left as you reach a gate at the end of the army ranges you will see a path leading down some steps (3). Take this and you will find yourself in the Fossil Forest. This is one of the highlights of the Jurassic Coast. The fossils here are known as stromatolites, and are the petrified remains of algal growths that colonised dead tree stumps. These Jurassic trees died over 100 million years ago as the sea level rose and the coastal swamps they lived in became too saline. Their leaves would have been munched by giant dinosaurs!

Return to the path and leave the ranges through the gate. You will shortly see a path on your right; follow this down to the beach and walk around the beach to the road which leads up to the Heritage Centre. Please note you may not be able to walk around the beach at high tide, so please check the tide times before the walk. The Heritage Centre has displays and information about the geography and geology of this famous location.

Above: A typical stromatolite from the Fossil Forest. The circular structure is a petrified ring of an algal growth that colonised the rotting tree stump. The hole in the centre shows where that tree stump once was.

Below: Mupe Rocks. The geology here is similar to that of Lulworth Cove (see page 34). The rocks are the steeply dipping Portland and Purbeck limestones.

Lulworth Cove (above) is world famous for its geology and hosts a constant stream of school, college and university field trips. The coastline here is said to be "concordant", meaning that the strata or layers of sedimentary rock run parallel to the direction of the coast. At the entrance to the cove the Purbeck and Portland limestones can be seen in steeply dipping layers, having been tilted and folded by giant earth movements. On top of, and therefore younger than, the Purbeck and Portland rocks lie soft Cretaceous sediments that were deposited in a giant delta, while at the back of the cove, again dipping steeply, is the Chalk.

After the Ice Age, a powerful river flowed down the valley now occupied by a small stream. It broke through the relatively hard limestones at the front of the cove allowing the sea to rapidly erode the softer sediments behind before coming up against the harder Chalk. This same pattern in the rocks can be seen in Mupe Bay, Worbarrow Bay and Swanage Bay, lying progressively to the east. However, as we go further east from Lulworth, the strata get thicker; thus at Swanage the wide sweep of the bay is formed from the softer sediments that form only a narrow part of the cliffs at Lulworth and are almost entirely pinched out at Durdle Door a little way to the west.

Povington Hill, Flower's Barrow, Worbarrow and Tyneham

A spectacular Iron Age hillfort. (SY 888812, BH20 5QN)

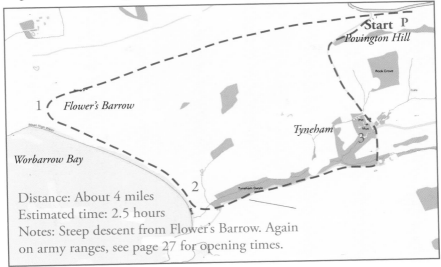

Distance: About 4 miles
Estimated time: 2.5 hours
Notes: Steep descent from Flower's Barrow. Again on army ranges, see page 27 for opening times.

The starting place for this walk is the large, free Whiteway Car Park on Povington Hill overlooking the deserted village of Tyneham (see also page 27). From the car park a footpath leads westwards along the Chalk ridge. Follow this until you reach Flower's Barrow (1). There is an Iron Age hillfort here – or at least half of one, half has disappeared due to cliff erosion. This is one of Dorset's many such hillforts, whose occupation ended with the Roman invasion of AD 43. From here follow the coast path down the steep scarp to Worbarrow Bay (2). This lovely bay is carved out of sands and clays sandwiched between the harder Portland and Purbeck limestones to the south and the Chalk to the north. For many years it supported a small fishing community until the area was requisitioned in 1943; ruins of some of its cottages can still be seen.

When you are ready take the track that leads inland along the valley to Tyneham (3) and have a good look around this deserted but atmospheric village, abandoned on the orders of the government in December 1943 so that it could form part of the training area for D-Day. It was mainly American forces that trained here; many of whom were involved in the fierce fighting at Omaha Beach. Today the village is a unique tourist attraction with many displays and information boards detailing the lives of its last inhabitants.

When you have finished here take the path that starts by a gate to the right (east) of the church. This will lead you back up Povington Hill where you should turn right and follow the path back to the car park.

Moreton and Clouds Hill (SY 826904, BH20 7NQ)
A beautiful church and memories of T. E. Lawrence.

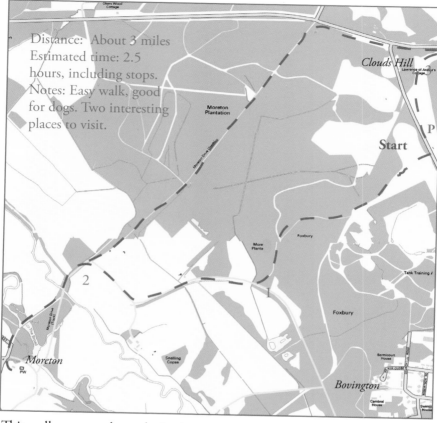

This walk starts at the tank viewing area just north of Bovington near Clouds Hill and Lawrence of Arabia's cottage (National Trust). The walk is part of the Lawrence of Arabia Trail and there are many signposts to help you navigate. On the other side of the road to the car park is a footpath leading over the heath. Take this and keep following the signs for the Lawrence of Arabia Trail, keeping right at the first junction (1) and left towards Moreton at the second (2). Follow the track to Moreton, over the lovely River Frome and be sure to pay a visit to Moreton Church. This was badly damaged by a stray bomb in World War II and its stained glass windows were destroyed. They were replaced by windows engraved by Laurence Whistler and the effect is stunning. A little further down the road on the other side is an extension of the cemetery which contains the grave of T.E. Lawrence.

Go back on the same path, across the River Frome and where the path branches (2) keep left for Clouds Hill. Follow this all the way to the road; turn right here and walk beside the road on the grass verge. A short way along, on the right, is the road to Bovington and just a little way down on the left is Lawrence of Arabia's cottage. It is owned by the National Trust and, although small, is a fascinating place to visit. Lawrence's fatal motorbike accident occurred a little further down the road. The path continues past the Bovington road and just as you reach the top of the hill you will see a sign on the right (3). Take this and follow the path back to the viewing area.

Above: The cottage of T.E. Lawrence at Clouds Hill. Left and below: Details from some of the marvellous engraved windows in the church at Moreton, the work of Laurence Whistler.

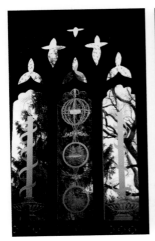

Church Knowle and Ridgeway Hill (SY 939818, BH20 5NF)
A beautiful Purbeck village.

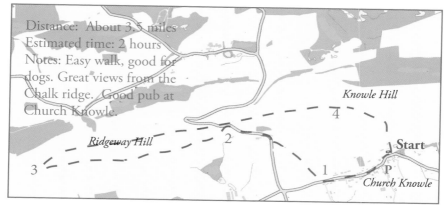

Distance: About 3.5 miles
Estimated time: 2 hours
Notes: Easy walk, good for dogs. Great views from the chalk ridge. Good pub at Church Knowle.

Right: There are amazing views from the ridgeway.

There are a few car parking spaces just to the west and opposite the church. From here walk westwards along the road, past the New Inn until you come to a playground on the right (1). Take the footpath that goes north and uphill from here. At the top left hand corner of the playground go over the stile and walk towards the top left hand corner of the next field. Here there is another stile; go over it and carry on in the same diagonal manner to the corner of this field, aiming for a cottage. Here go through the gate and follow the road uphill for a short while until you come to the top where the ridgeway path crosses the road (2). Go through the gate on the left but do not follow the ridgeway, instead follow the path on the left that goes down the slope a little way – this will lead you to the path along the bottom of the ridge. Keep to this for just over half a mile until it curves back up the ridge to your right (3). Take this path to the top of the ridge, go over the stile and turn right along the ridgeway. Keep going, over the small road you met earlier and just after a small information stone take the path on the right that goes diagonally down the ridge (4). Where this meets the path along the bottom of the ridge turn right towards Church Knowle and the starting point. You might want to end at the New Inn.

Wareham (SY 924872, BH20 4LP)

A historic town with a lovely quay on the River Frome.

Begin on the bridge over the Frome (1) facing north towards the town; take the first left along Abbot's Quay, following it round to the right where it becomes Tanners Lane. At the end turn left into Pound Lane; a little way along here is Castle Close and the mound you can see was where the Norman castle once stood (2). This saw action in the civil war between King Stephen and the Empress Matilda in the twelfth century. When you reach the end of Pound Lane cross the road and continue along the West Walls. These walls, now just a grassy bank, were built by the Saxons on the orders of Alfred the Great as defence against Viking raiders. Follow the walls to the right, now the North Walls and, at the end, turn right down North Street and make sure to visit St. Martin's Church (3) on the right at the top. This is a Saxon church built on the old Saxon walls. It is notable for medieval wall paintings and an effigy of Lawrence of Arabia. Turn right by the church along Lady's Walk and then left along St. Martin's Lane. At the end turn right onto the Town Walls. Follow the walk along the top of the walls, eastwards by a grassy area (4) then southwards. Cross over East Street and again follow the walls walk. Where the walls come to an end turn right into Conniger Lane, between two graveyards. Head towards St. Mary's Church (5) (well worth a visit) and then follow a sign from the green to the Quay and the bridge where the walk started. There are plenty of places to eat and drink.

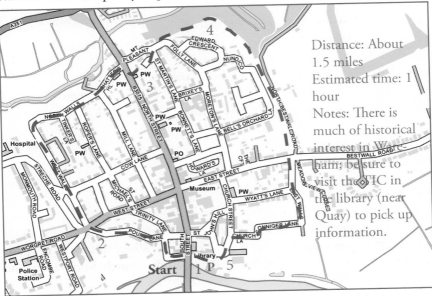

Distance: About 1.5 miles
Estimated time: 1 hour
Notes: There is much of historical interest in Wareham; be sure to visit the TIC in the library (near Quay) to pick up information.

Useful Information

There are Tourist Information Centres in Swanage and Wareham.
Wareham TIC - 01929 552740, e-mail tic@purbeck-dc.gov.uk
Swanage TIC - 01929 766018, e-mail mail@swanage.gov.uk

Swanage Town Council has a very informative website: www.swanage.gov.uk
Also see the very comprehensive website of Dorset councils:
www.dorsetforyou.gov.uk

For the RSPB Arne go to www.rspb.org.uk/reserves or phone 01929 553360

If you would like help planning your Purbeck holiday try Jurassic Jaunts,
www.jurassicjaunts.co.uk

Safety

- Please follow the Country Code and heed any warning signs.
- Keep away from cliff edges and from the bottom of cliffs, they can be unstable and rock falls are common. Keep a close watch on children and dogs under control.
- Do not climb or hammer the cliffs.
- Some of the walks have steep climbs or descents which can be slippery in wet weather - always have good footwear.
- Carry a map - the Ordnance Survey Outdoor Leisure 15 map covers all the walks in this book.

Front cover: The coast near Seacombe. Rear cover: The view from Houns-tout.